This book is dedicated to my children - Mikey, Kobe, and Jojo.

Copyright © 2024 Grow Grit Press LLC. All rights reserved. No part of this book may be reproduced in any form without permission in writing from the publisher. Please send bulk order requests to info@ninjalifehacks.tv

Paperback ISBN: 979-8-89614-015-3
Hardcover ISBN: 979-8-89614-017-7
eBook ISBN: 979-8-89614-016-0

Printed and bound in the USA.
NinjaLifeHacks.tv

Embarrassed Ninja

A Ninja's Guide to Overcoming Awkward Moments with Confidence

Ninja Life Hacks®
by Mary Nhin

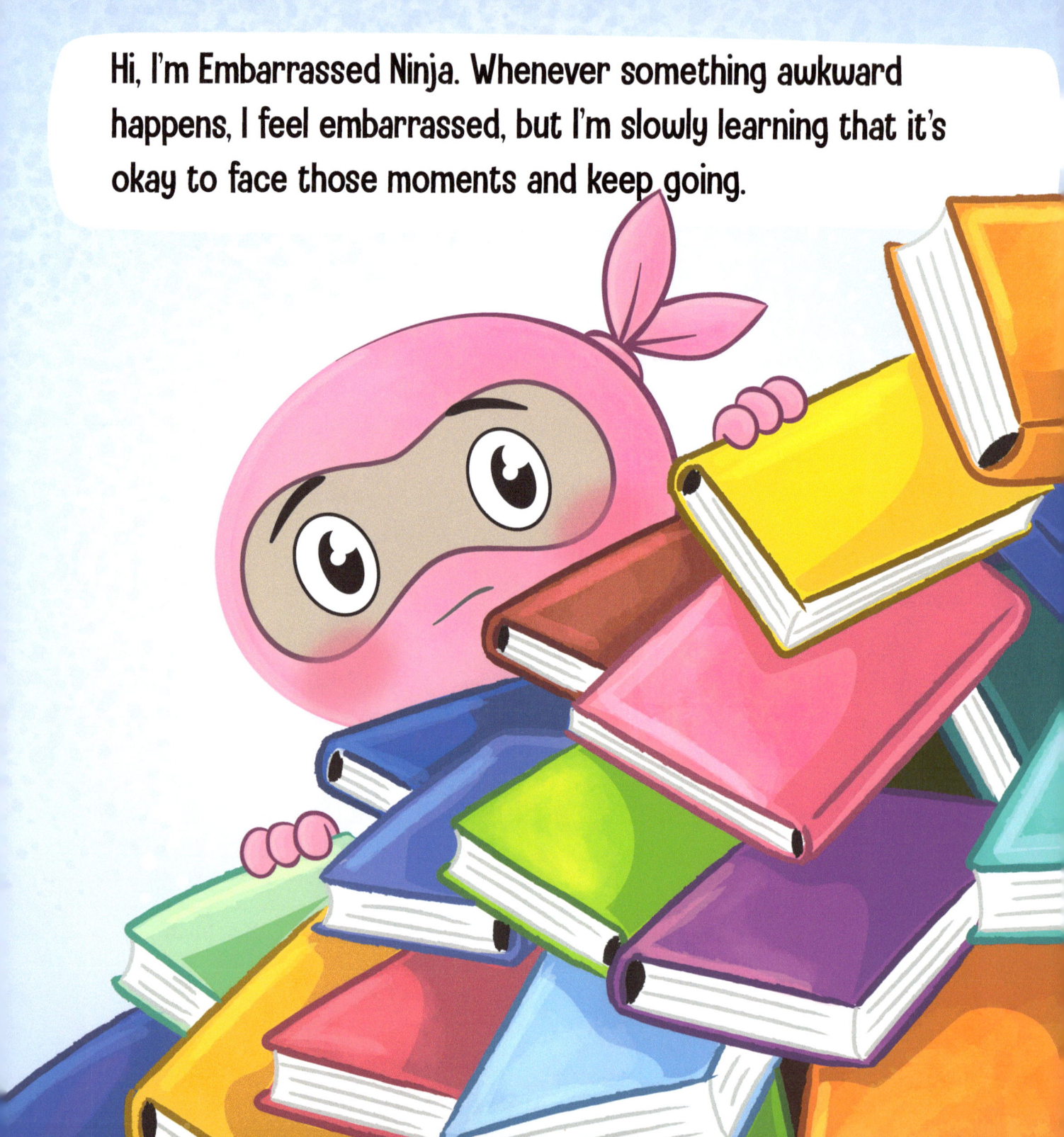

During a game, if I fall in front of everyone, I'm embarrassed, but I get up and keep playing. No one laughs, and I realize it's not so bad.

When the teacher calls on me, I get nervous, but I take a deep breath and give it my best shot. Even if I'm not sure, I try, and that's what matters.

For example, once at a party, I spilled my juice all over the table. I felt like everyone was staring at me.

At school, if I answered a question wrong, I would sink into my chair, feeling like I didn't belong. It made me want to stop trying.

But then one day, Confident Ninja shared a life hack with me on overcoming embarrassing situations.

It's okay to feel embarrassed, Embarrassed Ninja. We all feel that way sometimes. What counts is what you do in response to that feeling. I always remind myself to S.H.I.N.E.

S: Stop and Breathe- Pause and take a deep breath to calm your nerves.
H: Humor- Find the humor in the situation. Laughing it off can help reduce the tension.
I: Identify the Lesson- Reflect on what you can learn from the experience.
N: Normalize- Remind yourself that everyone makes mistakes and feels embarrassed sometimes.
E: Embrace the Moment- Accept the situation and move forward confidently, knowing it's a part of life.

This hack can help you **S.H.I.N.E.** through moments of embarrassment!

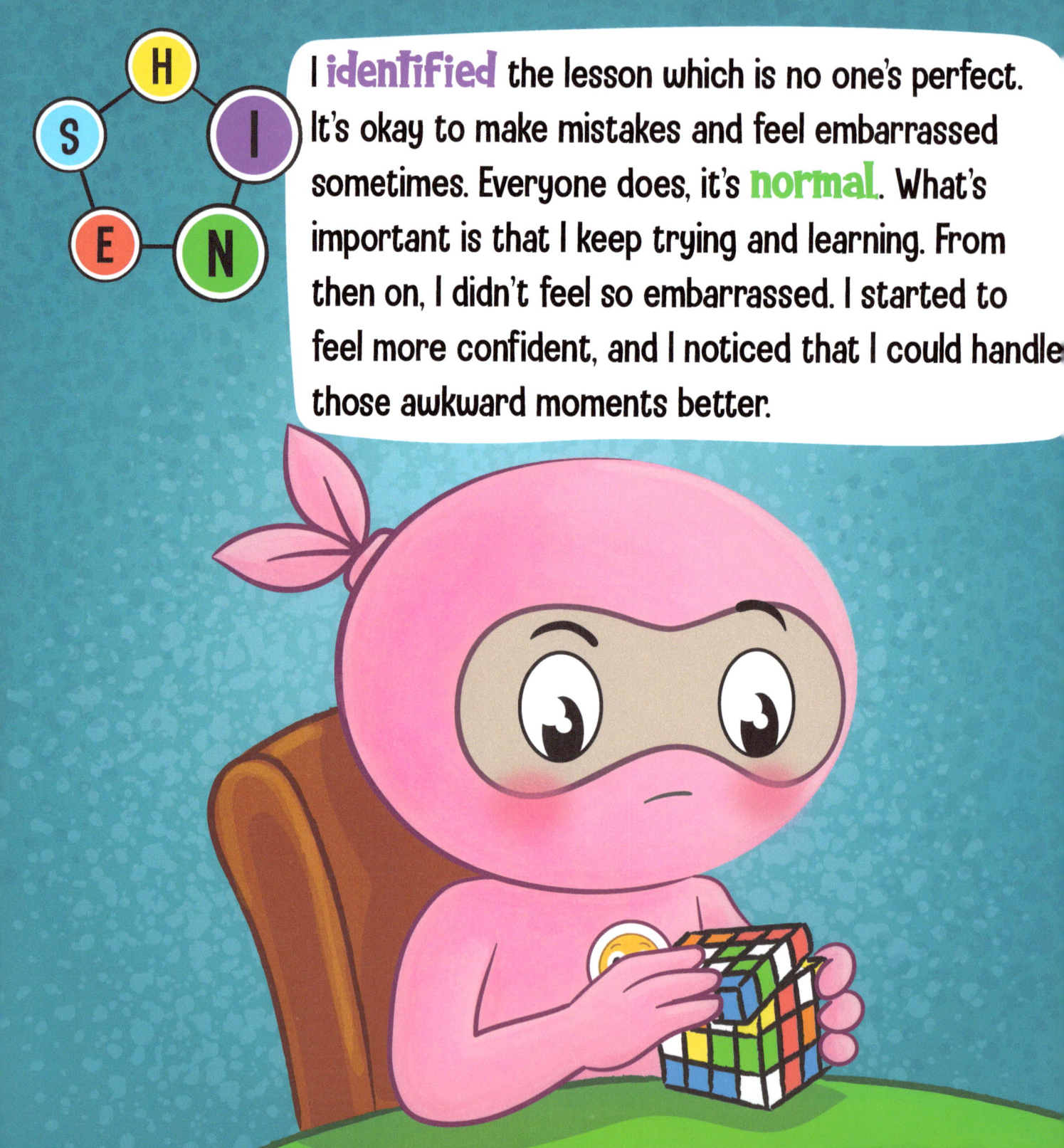

I couldn't believe I didn't feel as embarrassed anymore. I didn't think I could ever get over that hump.

S.H.I.N.E.

Check out the fun Embarassed Ninja lesson plans at ninjalifehacks.tv

I love to hear from my readers. Email me your feedback or thoughts on what my next story should be at info@ninjalifehacks.tv   Yours truly, Mary

 @marynhin   @GrowGrit   #NinjaLifeHacks

 Mary Nhin   Ninja Life Hacks

 Ninja Life Hacks

 @officialninjalifehacks

www.ingramcontent.com/pod-product-compliance
Lightning Source LLC
LaVergne TN
LVHW070435070526
838199LV00015B/517